CONTENTS

History of the Manor

A 15th Century wall painting of Richard Bluett, builder of the present house.

The origins of Cothay are lost in the mists of time. Most early medieval archives have long since disappeared. However, an early 13th century charter tells us that Richard, lord of Kydeford, granted to William de Cotthehee and his heirs, in return for his homage and services, one half virgate of land in Cotthehee within the manor of Kydeford, which William's ancestors had held from Richard's ancestors.

The language of this charter suggests that possibly the area of Cothay had been settled from before the Norman Conquest. Others also held land and dwellings at Cothay. In 1309 the delighfully named William Snyffmor and his wife Joan, granted all their lands and tenements at Cothay to three others, presumably trustees, for the rent of a double rose at Christmas and the Nativity of St John the Baptist (24th June). The impression, at this time, is of a small, tightly knit community living close to the river Tone. In 1309 William, great grandson of William de Cotthehee mentioned above, and son of Ralph de Cothay, granted a house measuring 43ft by 27ft to Thomas son of Lawrence the Smith of Greenham. The house was stated to lie between William's house and the hall of Adam de Cothay. Although there is no written evidence to support the existence of a high status predecessor of Cothay, there is architectural evidence of the existence of an early 14th century hall house incorporated into the 15th century house built by Richard Bluett.

Four more generations of de Cothays lived at Cothay. The last of the de Cothays, John, in 1457 transferred all their lands at Cothay to John Bluett and his son Walter. We do not know how the Bluetts came to own Kittesford and Greenham manors; whether by purchase or inheritance. It is known that the Bluetts were lords of the manor of Kittesford in 1342. The aforementioned John Bluett died in 1463 and was succeeded by his son Walter. Walter had two sons Nicholas, the elder, and Richard. Walter died in 1481 and Richard, the younger son, inherited Kittesford manor and all his father's land in Cothay. Richard Bluett apparently decided that the manor house of Kittesford was not sufficiently grand for himself and his family. He built the present house at Cothay from 1485 to 1488, undeterred by uncertainties following the victory of the future Henry VII over Richard III at the battle of Bosworth Field. Richard died in 1523 leaving two sons, Nicholas and Robert, and a daughter Anne.

Magnificent brasses in Kittesford church, where Richard and his wife Agnes are buried, depict him as clean shaven with shoulder length long wavy hair, parted in the middle and cut straight across the forehead. Richard's son Nicholas inherited Cothay and most of the manor of Kittesford. Nicholas died in 1549 and was succeeded by his eldest son, another Nicholas. Soon after Nicholas came into his inheritance, a manor court toll of 1558 indicated that the principal problems of the day were, as now, neglected roads, ditches, hedges and straying pigs. Nicholas died sometime soon after 1587 and John Bluett, the eldest of his five sons inherited. John, the last of the line of the builders of Cothay to live in the house, got himself heavily into debt, and to extricate himself from this burden he leased Cothay and the Kittesford avowson to Richard Weekes, his brother in law. Finally in 1605 Cothay was separated from the Kittesford estate and sold to William Every of Axminister, Devon. William added the dining room wing.

Tragically, William's wife, and his two sons, died before William. William died in 1652 and Cothay passed to his grandson, a further William. The tragedy of the Everys was to continue, for young William's three sisters were already dead and he died in 1660. In 1663 Cothay

passed to the old man's great-nephew, 17 year-old John. John spent little time at Cothay and died without issue, at the age of 35 in 1679. There follows a series of non-resident owners and the Every descendants conveyed Cothay away in 1796. Six years later John Cape became tenant of Cothay and his family farmed the land for the next 115 years.

The Sweet family, owners of Cothay from 1877, sold it to Lt. Col. Reginald Cooper, DSO in 1925; to Cooper fell the task of countering two and a half centuries of neglect, restoring the house to its former splendour. He uncovered a magnificent series of 15th century wall paintings, and a fresco of the same period. In twelve years he transformed what had become a run-down farmhouse into a national treasure. Reginald Cooper sold Cothay to Sir Francis Cook in 1937. Sir Francis was responsible for uncovering the wall painting in the Great Hall, adding the North Wing, taking a bend out of the river Tone, and rescuing the medieval deeds of Cothay which are now in the Somerset Record Office. In 1993 Cothay was bought by Alastair and Mary Anne Robb, who continue in Reginald Cooper's footsteps, to make Cothay and its garden a very special place to visit.

Cothay is entered through the ancient Gatehouse, originally castellated, though not fortified. In the 15th century, the Gatehouse was used as living accommodation for the servants. Now a one storied room, it is easy to see that the hall was originally divided into three stories. The higher the room, the higher the status of the servant. Passing through the Gatehouse to the porch, which is 1400, it is worth looking up and noticing the lead flying gutter, probably 15th century.

THE HOUSE
THE SCREENS PASSAGE

Before the Dining Room was added in the early 17th century, the Screens passage was a cross passage which led outside to a courtyard. The stone arch, on which the outside door hung, can still be seen as can the housing for the draw bar.

The floor of the passage is known as ashlar, made from river shale from the Tone, wood ash and lime. The five hundred year-old front door has its original wooden lockcase, wrought-iron handleplate, and ten and a half inch key. Cut into the door is a small round spy-hole. The straight staircase has replaced the much earlier spiral staircase, treads of which can be seen as you go up the stairs.

The Screens Gallery has a high wall of plastered lath, with a central wooden window with bars where women of the household would have been able to see what was going on in the Great Hall.

The Gallery had an architectural purpose, that of giving access to both sides of the house, but probably the most important purpose was as an extension to the very small oratory on the East wall, from where the household could attend daily prayers.

The Screens passage looking through to the dining room, added in the 17th century. The 15th century arch of the original outside door can be clearly seen.

THE GREAT HALL

The Great Hall follows the general development of the 15th century manor. The corbels of the massive trusses are wingless angels carrying shields. On the 12 angels' shields should properly be painted the coat of arms of the various owners of the manor. The roof reflects the spirit of the age in that the Bluetts were intent on creating an impression. The reverse wind-braces are an example of this, since conventional wind-braces would have been cheaper.

Until 1605, when the Everys added the dining room, the Great Hall would have been the centre of activity. On the raised dais, at the North end of the hall, would have been the high table. The squire, his lady and guests, would have sat here, with the rest of the household seated at the long table down the centre of the hall. On the parapet of the gallery can be seen the remnants of pegs which were used to rack halberds.

The transom windows, set high in the walls for security, have the pintles on which would have hung shutters. The bolt-holes still exist and these were sculpted from the same piece of stone as the mullion.

A wingless angel holding a shield on the corbel of a truss.

A 17th century tabernacle frame
with a 19th century painting of the
Crucifixion. Artist unknown.

The oak panelling was added by the Everys in 1605. It is
most unusual because, like that in the Long Gallery at
Haddon Hall in Derbyshire, it has been painted to look like
walnut. The mouldings of the panels were gilded, traces of
which remain.

The walls of medieval houses were brightly decorated. Here,
at Cothay, uncovered in the 1930s, the allegorical scene of
the funeral of Reynard the fox being hung by two geese on
a gibbet, is still faintly visible. Apart from the predominantly
17th century furniture, the hall must look much as it did
when Richard Bluett built it in 1485 to impress his friends
and neighbours.

It is said that on a cold, windy night the sound of a dog's
claws, clicking on the stone floor as he makes his way across
the hall, can be heard above the wind.

The smell of beeswax, and wood smoke from the fire, mingling with the life
of this ancient house, create an atmosphere of past times – adding to the
feeling that little has changed since the time of Richard Bluett.

A French 15th century Romane panel

11

THE WINTER PARLOUR

The winter parlour, entered from the great hall through a double ogee door, would in 1485, as other rooms, have been brightly painted.

The remnant of the wall painting above the wainscoting, to the left of the window, is possibly a scene from the parable of the prodigal son. The wooden transom window was added later in about 1558. The panelling, put in by the Everys in 1609 is the same as that in the Great Hall. The sprung ceiling is of moulded and pegged oak beams. The curtains, like most of the hangings in the house, are made from cloth woven locally by Christopher Elvy, recreating many old designs. A hidden spiral staircase, behind the panelling, leads to the Great Chamber above.

THE DINING ROOM

The Dining Room added by William Every in 1609 - panelled in oak, the top of which is linenfold, with a fine carved chimney piece on which the arms of the Every's are impaled with that of Haydon, two shields being left partially blank for future generations.

The four carved figures are of Plato's Cardinal Virtues – Justice, Fortitude, Temperance and Prudence. The original paintwork is still clearly visible. The stone fireplace has a very rare carving of a six pointed star – which in 17th century England was said to stop witches from coming down the chimney.

The decoration of the ceiling is of local plasterwork, carved in situ with a design of vine leaves and grapes. In each corner are sculptured heads, possibly portraying the craftsmen involved in the construction of the dining room wing.

The furniture in this room is 18th century. The pattern on the heavy wool curtains is taken from a piece of material found on a bed cover at nearby Cothele.

One of the 12 different plaster sculptures to be seen in each corner of the panelled ceiling.

Detail of 17th century chimneypiece on facing page. The first shield carved with the arms of Every (or, four chevronels gules) impaling those of Haydon, William's wife (argent, three gemelles azure, on a chief gules a fesse dancettee or); the remaining two shields are left partially blank - presumably to record marriages of future generations.

THE GOLD ROOM

So-called because of particles of medieval gold paint which were found on the walls.
Originally a sleeping chamber, the room has the only fresco in the house, depicting the
Madonna and Child, (the colours still bright and fresh though painted 500 years ago), in
front of a landscape with buildings contained in a roundel. In the top left hand corner is
a shield, with the Bluett eagle displayed, top right with the Verney quatrefoil device. In
the 1930s an eminent professor restored the fresco with the most modern technology of
the time, which was to inject wax behind the plaster. Sadly, this had the effect of lifting
the fresco from the wall
when the wax melted,
due to the sun streaming
through the south light.

The chamber is now an
ante-room, with an oak
table made in Exeter in
1600. The walls are
decorated with family
photographs, letters and
autographs, among them
a postcard from William
Gladstone and a letter
from Charles Kingsley.

19

THE ORATORY

The Oratory, over the porch, faces east towards Jerusalem. This tiny chapel measures 9 x 8 foot. The altar cloth, made from a bishop's cope, is of yellow embroidered Spittalfield silk. The cross originally covered in carved mother of pearl, is 17th century Spanish colonial from Cuzo in South America. Two medieval stone angels hang from beam ends. On either side of the door are two oak chairs bearing the date 1713. The kneelers in front of the altar were embroidered recently by Margaret Cothay. They are of Talbots, medieval hunting dogs, now extinct, surrounded by flowers – the design inspired by a Cluny tapestry. In the 15th century, lay prayer was becoming increasingly popular, prayers would have been said daily, in the absence of the priest, by the lord of the manor, taken from a Book of Hours. Here, on the lectern, the book is a copy of the *Great Book of Hours* made for the Duc du Berry by the Limbourgh brothers in the 15th century. The two putti, carved in Venice by the well-known Venetian gilder, Gianni Cavalier, hang to the side of the altar on the east wall. This lovely oratory, now much in use, was blessed after its restoration by a great friend of the family, Father John Tranmar, S.J.

The Oratory as seen from the Screens Gallery.

THE GUEST CHAMBER

The Guest Chamber with its 15th century frieze of ribbon pattern, interspersed with writing, still faintly visible. Uncovered in the 1920s are the wall paintings. To the left of the window is an Annunciation. The Christ Child is descending on a ray of light from the Godhead, the lily, towards the Virgin Mary. This iconographical representation of the Incarnation suggested that the body of Jesus was not formed in the Virgin's womb. This heresy persisted until banned by Pope Benedict XIV in the 18th century. To the right of the window, another wall painting shows a woman in a close fitting coif, and halo, standing in the centre looking left and downwards with an elderly bearded man kneeling behind her. This probably represents Our Lady and St. Joseph. To the left of the fireplace, a male secular figure in costume of the period *c.*1580, is possibly a portrait of Richard Bluett, the builder of Cothay.

 The sprung ceiling, with its moulded beams, is otherwise unadorned. In the corner of the chamber a hagioscope looks through to the altar in the adjoining oratory, which is connected by a small door. The room haunted with visits on occasions by the apparition of a monk.

THE BOOK ROOM

The Book Room painted red and overlaid with a darker colour, matches the colour of the stained glass window which bears the coat of arms of Sir Francis Cook Bart.,

with the motto '*esse quam vedere*'. Sir Francis, a colourful character, lived at Cothay during the Second World War.

This small chamber, with its unsophisticated ceiling, may have been part of an earlier dwelling, incorporated into the main house by Richard Bluett in 1485 and used perhaps as a summer parlour as it has no fireplace. Of interest in the room are two 17th century portraits painted on leather. A rare 18th century Khasa, which is a Buddhist monk's robe made of silk, still retains its original straps to keep it in place – now used as a table cloth.

THE
GEORGIAN
HALL

The Georgian Hall connects the old
house with Sir Francis Cook's 1938
North Wing. It was so-called
because of the fine staircase of 1732,
taken from a nearby house before it
was demolished.

The walls are of local cob and the
floor of limestone flags. The
portrait is of George Henry
Boughton R.A., (1833 - 1905) in
fancy dress, painted by John Pettie
R.A., (1839 - 1893).

As you climb the staircase you can
see the original outside wall of the
old house where the bargeboard
and gutter brackets are still visible.

THE GREAT CHAMBER

The Great Chamber or Withdrawing Chamber was a private bed-sitting room of the squire and his family.

The roof is of splendid oak beams. The high occulus window is said to be 14th century, probably from an earlier building, the hall house of Adam de Cothay. Overlooking the Great Hall is a squint for the squire to communicate with the hall. The transom windows are pre-1480. Medieval houses, contrary to common opinion, were brightly painted. Between Henry VIII and Cromwell, eighty per cent of English art was destroyed. The King of France in early medieval times had his favourite hunting forest painted on the walls of a chamber. Here in the Great Chamber, the walls have been painted by Arabella Arkwright with stylised flowers.

The furniture and objects of virtue are an eclectic mix, mostly 18th century.

Florentine glass

28

THE GARDENS

The garden, laid out off a 200 yard yew walk in the 1920s by Colonel Reginald Cooper D.S.O. (Harold Nicholson of Sissinghurst's oldest friend and a friend of Lawrence Johnstone of Hidcott and the Architect Edwin Lutyens), was gutted in the early 1990s within the original framework. The restoration and additions to the garden have so far taken ten years and are an on-going project.

Cothay is a romantic garden epitomised by the terrace on which is planted a Red Rose for York and a White for Lancaster. Legend has it that here, planted to celebrate the end of the Wars of the Roses in the 15th century when Richard Bluett built Cothay, they have always flowered. Off the long yew walk are many small garden rooms, further enclosed by yew hedges. Like the rooms of the house they have their own individual character.

Cothay is predominantly a summer garden, at its best from May when thousands of white lily-flowered tulips herald the season, like an army of white angels marching through the garden. For in the summer months the glory of this ancient place is at its best.

The **Green Knight Garden**, named after one of King Arthur's knights, planted in silver and white surrounding an oblong lawn, flowers from May

until the autumn. The **Bog Garden**, made from the old river course with giant stepping stones, is filled with gunneras, irises, primuli and large leafy plants looking

lovely in early Summer. The **Herbaceous Borders** planted with pale colours under an English sky hold their own until August. In **Emily's Garden** is the old Kentucky bean tree *gymnocladus*, the beans of which were used by the early settlers to make coffee. It does not set seed here and seldom flowers except in a very hot summer. In this garden the colours are yellow and cream, starting with the single pale yellow *paeonia mlokosewitschii* ~ known as '*Molly the Witch*'. Opposite is the **Cherry Garden** where the lovely early *Prunus 'Ukon'* shades the garden throughout the summer months and shade-loving plants predominate. The **Bishop's Room** where the colours are episcopal purple and scarlet. The **Cottage Garden** full of sweet peas. The **Courtyard** reflects the colour of the old harling on the walls with the colour of late summer sunsets, apricots and oranges. The new **Walk of the Unicorn** with the stone statue of a captive unicorn, his bronze horn shimmering in the moonlight. The **New Pond** in the shape of a tear drop - each year new projects making the garden a never-ending joy to visit.

To conjure, even for a moment, the wistfulness which is the past is like trying to gather in one's arms the hyacinthine colour of the distance. But if it is once achieved, what sweetness! Like the gentle fugitive fragrance of spring flowers, dried with bergamot and bay. How the tears will spring in the reading of some old parchment - 'to my dear child, my tablets and my ring' - or of yellow letters, with the love still fresh and fair in them though the ink is faded - 'and so goodnight, my dearest heart, and God send you happy'. That vivid present of theirs, how faint it grows. The past is only the present become invisible and mute, its memoried glances and its murmurs are infinitely precious. We are tomorrow's past. Even now we slip away like those pictures painted on the moving dials of antique clocks - a ship, a cottage, sun and moon, a nosegay. The dial turns, the ship rides up and sinks again, the yellow-painted sun has set, and we that were the new things, gather magic as we go.

MARY WEBB, PRECIOUS BANE
1920